<u>Walking the line.</u>

The high speed rail two project (HS2) is an over costed, environmentally destructive vanity project that has been a dirty black hole in the British peoples finances for some years now.

*The HS2 plot was started in 2009,
the government set up a company
with all the powers of the government,
powers to arbitrarily claim land
public treasury funded
but. <u>limited responsibility</u>
and was enshrined in the law
by a three party whip in parliament
a vote where MPs don't get to vote..
If you're confused. That's intentional.*

Between the destruction on our landscapes, the monumental land grab, the irreparable damage to critical water infrastructure and the phenomenal amounts of money, dedicating myself to ensuring this project comes to an end with the minimum of negative long term consequences for future generations is an occupation I can be proud of.

*The poet is a woodland ecologist, anarchist,
part time hippy and registered existential threat to the establishment.*

These are some poems from within the stop HS2 movement.

<u>*A Crumb of Context?*</u>

These poems were written to be performed either for contractors, protestors or the police; audiences where additional context was not required.
(In theory, the constabulary can be a little slow to catch on)

We were living a rather <u>unnormal</u> life, we lived in tents on sites where the bailiffs might turn up and smash all our stuff. But we did morning meditations and workshops about how to build resilient loving communities, we taught kids to climb and had incredible people teach the community about bats and birds and the laws on squatting

We were transient, moving between the impromptu camps, tight knit groups interlocking with a wider community of hundreds of people with a huge diversity of backgrounds, beliefs, traumas and tactics

We made pallet walls and wrapped them in barbed wire, we fed the masses out of the bins, we built tree houses you could live in for a month without ever touching the ground. Getting up at 6 to dress as a bat and jump a fence, was an average Tuesday.

If we were digging holes, planting seeds, hanging banners or surfing trucks it was all done with the energy and purpose of people willing to face insurmountable odds because it's the right thing to do.

All my thanks to the amazing people that make up the #Stophs2 movement and #hs2rebellion. Trying to thank such a mixed and eclectic group of people willing to live within a semi-intentional, unstructured, semi-legal, high pressure environment to put their heart and soul into protecting the landscape that bore us. is truly inspiring, A large collection of very good eggs.

A Billion Pounds A Mile

A billion pounds a mile, I'll let that sink in.
without a calculator I'm pretty sure you could,
pave the way in silver blocks, six inches thick.
engraved by master craftsmen, and laid on a goose feather bed
you could have a fountain of wine
at every single village
between Birmingham and London

You could run my town for a thousand years
but rather than do that,
we'll save you twenty minutes a day
pay a few people millions
and burn down our oldest forest.

A billion pounds a mile, walk that then come tell me
what you think you could do, to make that mile better
would you steal peoples land, fence it off and kill the bats
would you rip up all the soil and move it round in dumper trucks?

With a billion pounds a mile, what do you think you can do?
you can permeate the water tables, that have fed us ten thousand years
you can desecrate the graveyards
commit violence against the plebs
rewrite all the laws
fill your pockets deep
you can promise anything
unicorn rides to the moon
hire an army of black clad goons
to beat hippies out of trees.

With a billion pounds a mile, what can we do?
we can make two billion, we'll call it HS2
we'll write a dodgy contact, get it signed by someone posh
max out all the overtime, overrun the costs
give them no other options
make' em throw good money, after bad
we can double our money
and grab the land.

A billion pounds a mile, can make you richer than God
you can hide it all in bank accounts and watch those numbers swell

or, if you would
entertain another idea
just give it all away, to the people that really need it
give nature a bit of a break
and pay, let's say,
everyone's wages, around two thirds
for a yearlong holiday.
You could reopen all the libraries
give milk back to the kids
or a soy alternative if that's their parents thing
you could reopen homeless shelters
that have recently disappeared
you could actually run some transport
to those villages isolated
by austerity and economics
from when we bailed out the banks
and kicked that massive bubble down
to a time that's now

A billion pounds a mile, measure that by the inch,
it's a long way over what I make in a year
and honestly I do fine
I'm warm and I'm fed,
I have water to drink, clothes on my bed.
With a billion pounds a mile you can sufficiently sort
all the people living to properly ensure
they have what they need
and don't fall into
the depression and stress
the financial system
places on the people

A billion pounds a mile is fifty pound notes
all stacked on their thin side, in two long neat rows
with still enough left over, to power us by the sun
and do our part, to part our way
from the oil that's done us no good
we could feed all the starving children
in every corner of the world
maybe not forever, but certainly for a week

With a billion pounds a mile we can repair all our seas,
clean up all the plastic, save all the bees
with a billion pounds a mile we could strike a balance
between food and fallow,
commerce and calm places
and grow what we need in harmony
because that's not currently how we do it

With a billion pounds a mile, some thought and without greed.
we could make almost everyone happy
some people are never pleased

This magic golden railway
that I presume is going to be free
isn't worth the money
and it certainly isn't worth the grief

<u>A Billion Pounds A Mile.</u>

So yeah, That.
I've done some heavy rounding, (poetic licence and all that) but I'm actually pretty
sure the costs are going to rocket past, I am already planning the "two billion a
mile"
It's about 120 miles, Birmingham to London (Phase 1 of 1) the idea that there is ever
any London centric demand to connect the north is a fucking joke. Ask pretty
much ANYONE in the north, we know it and we don't care. But don't try and add
miles so it seems more cost effective, Cheeky bastards.
They might be stealing land, but they won't be laying rails.

They are paying 100 grand quotes for a days work with a digger. Paying to put
fences to nowhere. Money is being haemorrhaged into non-jobs and it's not the poor
mug doing the pointless digging that's getting rich.

At I think currently 108 billion it's almost a billion quid a mile.
that's a lot of zeros. Like your brain doesn't get it.

A million seconds ago was last week.
A billion seconds ago was the year I was born.

H2O NOT HS2

Aqua vitae, rain and stream
it falls from the sky, and it works its way in
though air and leaves, and forest floor
filtered through soil, transpired through pores.
all life as we know it, relies on this flow.

We stand in a land where the droughts are expanding
two months, three, how long until famine

We all gladly accept, the reasonable measures
Perhaps your lawn, does not need those sprinklers
So we turn off the tap while brushing our teeth
And you have a dishwasher that works less than the sink
Shorter showers to deny our meditations
During the sacred ceremony of our daily cleansings
and yet, my kin, gather all around
I will tell you a story, common in this land
It's one rule for us, another for them.

There is a beast that stands, with a thousand legs,
and a thousand pounds a moment,
each coin extracted, from your back pocket
it thieves all your water from your floral borders
to spray across the landscape it's raped and pillaged
to muffle her cries of complaint
that manifest in dust clouds
that obscure your view
and leave a film on your windscreen
that was once, the very earth
we should never have seen.

How can we be so meek
when such a tragedy adds insult to injury
how can we be so calm
when another million gallons is stolen from us

Perhaps its value has been diminished
by the ease of accessibility
the primary, number one, basic essential
siphoned away from the public
to business

This isn't this beasts' only crime,
this mischief is a compounded effect.
this beast is so set, on making desert
oh Britain, our green and pleasant land,
cut away delinquently, one line at a time
despite increasing knowledge,
that trees and soil are intrinsic
to the bottom blocks, upon which we build
the idol of modern society.

The crawling, driving, drivelling beast
with its thousand eyes and gloved clenched fists
isn't concerned with the greater world,
only the line between central and capital
to save its captives a mere 20 minutes,
displaces the rights, these trees once held sacred
the rights that belong to our landscape heritage
cast aside, on the altar of corporatism

H20 not HS2, we have need to increase the speed
and save us all,
a rivers worth of water,
that falls from the sky,
as a gift
from nature
to us all.

During a dry spell in early summer the woodland and farmland sites from which the works had removed the topsoil from baked pretty hard in the sun. After not too long dust clouds started bothering people in the local town, leaving a gritty film on windows and causing breathing problems for workers.. So, the response was to cover the [However many] square miles in sprinklers. moving all the water in via trucks. Spraying it into the sun. Idiots

Also sort of comparing the HS2 ltd to the east India corporation that sort of started the age of corporatism that the modern world was planted in. There is a lot of pretending that things don't work like that anymore, with private armies running the world at the barrel of a gun, but the mechanisms for removing the rights of anyone that stands in the way seems to be pretty effective in the modern age. Paper companies get to basically shit all over actual humans and that's all fine... apparently.

I suppose one shouldn't complain
Oppressions better than execution, right?

<u>Seven Singing Girls</u>

I have slept in moonlight by singing at the fire,
in a place of free expressions and synchronicities.
elated to stand with comrades
of all ages and creed and kind
balanced by paranoia
that bailiffs in black provide

Sharing and supporting
all that hippy stuff
wraps you in security
and makes you stronger still

Today we travelled to see sisters
we had yet to meet
to picnic under an oak
that kites and bats frequent
how rudely we were handled
by the second wave of law
when they decided to send a score and some
to steal seven singing girls.

<u>Seven Singing Girls</u>

Originally, I counted six and wrote the poem but there were seven.
it goes much better if there were six.
grumble

Yeah, bastards.
Police sent 30 odd officers to drag off 7 women sat under a tree to stop the illegal
dismantlement of it.

It's a 100% no-no sort of tree,
veteran in a field landscape, full of bats, holds the corner of the stream together, has
a larger variety of undergrowth due to the shade it casts and the "seed-rain",
higher moisture in the air, evapotranspiration, mycelium communities, the benefits
are mature trees are critical, manifold and painfully overlooked

No problems for the company doing the illegal shit.
Just nick the hippies stopping them.
#Sevensistersoak

Funnily enough it was afterwards taken out of the plans
However that is another story

Impartial policing, sponsored by HS2.

<u>Our Sisters Tree</u>

They came again, for our sisters tree
that we once fought, to keep in seed
no law or right written
by man or community
gives anyone the right
to lay low our eldest oak

We cried havoc, but were faced with arms
our peaceful protest,
found no grip
when the constabulary
turned up with grins
and claimed there was never a tree
no shade or leaf or woody stem
it was always chip, says the man with the chipper

The paper logs in digital form
say the survey was done at dawn
but the sun knows
the chains arrived at 9
and they didn't even look
till the dawn song was sung

The paper logs in digital form
say an inspector was there
and it was all above board
however that can't really be
as I was stood where he claimed to be.

I was told by phone
he was stood beside me
and it was no problem
the man with the chipper pays him
but this spectral officer was never there
despite the logs and police claims
Chief inspector Parsons is either made from air
or willing to write lies
to help men feather his nest.

<u>Our Sisters Tree</u>

So while the tree talked about in the seven singing girls poem was still evidence in
an ongoing police investigation the national eviction team (the militia answerable
to the minster of transport) came with their 40 strong mob and a chainsaw team to
come and destroy the tree.
they spent the whole day standing on our fence line looking at the camp, they
didn't seem to like the look of the tower and after they had destroyed the
tree/evidence/habitat/heritage they left...

..and evicted half of Jones hill wood the next day
the one Roald Dahl wrote Fantastic Mr Fox about.

Fucking police lying on the logs about being there, ecology surveys, refused access
to any other police officers so no wildlife crime officer.

Bull. Shit.

So yeah Chief inspector Henry Parsons, you are a fucking liar.
But I'm sure you sleep sound when HS2 are paying off your mortgage

Lesser Harmony

If you take the seashells the world sounds very different.
Unlike common music, discordance can be born, of a lacking
while the song of the world marches on
a sudden seeing that the notes
might not meld as they could

If the Mona Lisa were to lose a lash
would her smile become obvious at last
if you took Morgana, out from Arthurs tale
if you took the mirrors, from a mirrored maze
once you take an aspect, It ceases to be what it was
whenever faces change, there is a sense of loss.

Lesser Harmony

Written on the bus ride back from everyone getting nicked. It was quiet and grim.

Activism tends to create strong units of really capable people helping each other in a networked, skill sharing, group responsibility setting whilst still keeping our individualism and the right to protest how we each feel is best.

When the dynamics of a group change it very much changes the tone of things. sometimes it's a bit glum.

<u>Self-Appointed Spot.</u>

When falling from our responsibilities
that we have shouldered ourselves
the view down is a kaleidoscope
of all your ignored pains

The fall from grace is a trickster
that turns the world on its' head
says friends conspired against you
and passing smiles are smirks

Once you have fallen
from your self-appointed spot
you feel you're failing others
and they expect too much
but where the others are standing
is underneath you and prepared
to catch you while you're falling
and take you safely to bed.

Catching those who are falling
is the occupation of the age
now the world around us
is falling like dominoes

You will find yourself on waking
the weight has moved away
onto the backs of others
and the campaign carries on
then you can breathe and rest

Ready to do your best
and catch the next one falling
hold them and say
you're safe.

Camp and community life can be difficult, it's predominantly extremely rewarding and allows people to really thrive, but particularly within informal communities people can take on roles and get stuck with them, or find that they become the go-to person for much more than they would like.
This causes burn outs and often people step out and do some regen (regen is important)

I always find it pretty inspiring how we always seem to muddle on through with transient anarchist spaces, sometimes the washing up just does itself. Powerful places.

<u>Thor Water.</u>

I heard Thor cheer as he sent a week of rain
precious and permeating ,
Through covers onto skin
the energy is high
and the foundations are deep
deeper still by every shovel
and swing of the pick
the strength of peace is inspiring
despite the occasional strife
could you resist your violence
against a man who broke your son?

With rope and canvas and beating hearts,
against governance and finance,
lies and rigged votes
forest, glade, stream and lake
upon the ground where children once played

An eclectic mix of people and skill
working in unison
to save what's still left of
the wildwood we wandered
before numbers became the focus
of a society
where people feel
the hole inside
can be filled with money.

<u>Verity's 12th</u>

I visited a wood in which I'd once lived
to gift a charm to a child I had grown to love
carved with Odin, Frey and Thor
and carried carefully down the path of our war.

These woods are not like others you know
its' community insists on repairing the earth
as a group that forsakes the principles
of the wider worlds' rush for money

By hand and horse, and sweat of brow
they live a different kind of hurry
not enslaved by the tyranny of the clock
to sign in by nine or risk losing your job
their shifts are decided by the growing of grass
Minute by minute matters less
than the path of the sun
and the seasons it brings

But even this enclave of ecoists isn't immune
from conflict that government propaganda sneaks in
to divide up people and start discussions
that end in vicious defence
of personal opinions

<u>Verity's 12th</u>

Visited a place I used to live called Tinkers Bubble and headed there for one of the kids' birthdays, bit of a more eclectic mix of people than usual and during the early days of the covid propaganda really getting hammered in. Very heated discussions ensued.

Coming off the camps where discussions between people with very different views take place in a learning and enlightening manner., it was a reminder that it doesn't work like that everywhere. A major problem in our age is the vicious defence of personal opinions. All it takes is an attitude change to make most of our arguments into lessons., wider community doesn't meld like that, our camps were nailing it.

Tinkers is a zero fossil fuel community with an orchard, gardens and woods. An inspirational place when thinking of alternative futures away from the dying beast that is the great global capitalism machine.

Hard graft that place.

<u>The Violence Of Progress</u>

The violence of our progress is calamitous
its' giddy plans so thoughtless it's sick
not a thought of how the land lies
when your pet machine moves it in an instant

The violence of our progress is dangerous
we upset balances we barely know
we're draining the soil of nutrients
until yields drop to zero

The violence of our progress is increasing
with faster heavier machines
and intruding into the world of DNA
and modified protein
the violence of our progress is new
in only 10,000 years

we have strangled the earth with road and rail
and poisoned all the seas
we've slashed and burned the savannah
attacked the artic with drills

If we carry on this way
there will be nowhere for us
to live

<u>Ecocide Is Suicide</u>

Ecocide is suicide. By any other name.
Burning the foundations of our ivory towers
Ecocide is suicide. On a global scale.
Burning through soil and poisoning the streams
Ecocide is suicide. Over many years.
Starting with any life we failed to utilise
Ecocide is suicide. Decided by few for all.
The madness of believing money can fix the earth

Ecocide is suicide. Not just for bees, for us.
And almost all the creatures, with their back to the sun
Ecocide is suicide. I will say it till I'm hoarse.
I'll shout it from street corners, until we change course
Ecocide is genocide. It's murder with intent.
Violation of the landscapes and violence disguised as progress
Ecocide is genocide. And with no doubt it's a crime.
That is committed and defended, by those who hold the cards.

Ecocide is simple. It happens every day.
with every field and forest, that we scrape away
Ecocide is simple. And slowly at first.
the buzz of spring, begins to need, strained ears to hear
species over the globe, begin to disappear
millions of generations of life and harmony
destroyed in mere moments
by mechanised industry

<u>Ecocide Is Suicide</u>

a term defined recently as a move to try and criminalise the destruction of land and ecosystems. Look it up. I'm not your fucking science teacher.

Because currently destroying the very web of life that has supported and sustained us since we climbed out the proverbial primordial soup isn't a crime.

We are probably fucking doomed.

People have a minimal understanding about how critical life is to life, modern schooling, buildings, roads, sterile concrete. We have been raised far removed from it. We are destroying the things we need to survive.

The Grove

How do we tame a beast, that's lived a thousand years
that's chewed up all our parents, and a hundred generations before.
its cells are made from naked apes, Its nerves are made of wire.
it's grown sick whilst its' filaments, reach every corner of the globe.

Bring me all your malcontents, rebels and subversives
gather up the outcast, the queer and the weird
I'll lead us to the Avon where the water moves like wind
hide us in the nettle patch, protected from the stings
we can befriend the dragonfly, and live amongst the yew
we can cut ourselves a grove, and begin council anew

Society spreads like mycelium, Its' fibres road and rail
and now it is essential to change how it behaves.
over are the days, where the wood beat the axe
by growing a little faster
than man can drag by horse
humanity is reaching maturity,
childish things must be lost
like drawing ever more borders
and chasing eternal growth.

Terra is our terrarium
and now it's filled with us,
this path that we are headed down,
is doomed to crack the glass
there are no more lands to conquer
there is no more room to spread
we need a new council
and a new way to exist.

<u>What If?</u>

What if we lived in a world, where who owns what was very different
where no house has a lock but everyone does the laundry
a bothy home every quarter mile
some of them vacant, Some of them full.

What if we lived in a world where strangers came for tea,
told you how the road was and passed out in the spare room
and they always cut the firewood, or tended to the kids
depending on what it was ,they thought they could do to help.

What if we lived in world, where you picked apples all the day
chatted, danced and sang, then gave them all away
and everyone trusted each other, to leave each other a share
but when it didn't happen, it wasn't the end of the world

What if your dinner was what was in reach
and nobody really cared who cooked it
or what portions it was in and everything was free
we could do away with money!

I'm sure some things might fade away,
like fast cars, banking tzars, satellites
and suicides
but all we need is abundant
It's in the nature that's all around us.

What if nobody cared who the dad was
and every maid was the mother
and if you found a child crying
you'd tend it as you should

So what if the roads get wrecked, there is a bed every click
if it bothers you that much then fix it,
some people will be ecstatic
what if we lived in a world where nobody owned anything
and sharing didn't have to be a word,
because it's just what we did.

<u>The Nettle Stings</u>

Yes I know that I have no shoes on
but the nettle stings
don't bother me nearly as much as your presumptions
that you have any right
to tell me how to live my life
or what attire should be on
my little pink toesies

No, I don't mind the bramble patch,
each of my steps in considered
and when I feel a slug slide its' last between my toes
at least I am aware of the things that die
beneath my stride

The stick I carry is a flag and a home
it keeps me and mine sheltered and keeps us safe on the roads
your stick however provides no such benefits
it is purely for violence and compliance

So perhaps officer you could readdress
to whom to who is a protentional threat
and understanding peaceful people doing what people do
is not a problem for you to solve
by persecuting, someone weird

I may be in the road but all it means is people slow
my flag creates safety and maybe a spectacle
but we mean no distress
and legally can progress

Despite some alarm by the less travelled of the population
all I'm doing is traveling the country
to enjoy the walk and converse with the crows
I cannot do that at 60
In fact any of the limits that are targets for motorist
Is a pace I find quite anxious

The speed today paced by a man with a flag
three horse two bike some people and a dog
is a pace that's just about perfect
to enjoy nature

I may have caused a backup
but you will have to excuse me
I'm carrying my home
in this bag wrapped around me

So again I will stress
no matter what you think is best
we are living differently
away from fast cars and money,
now thank you for the concern,,
I understand we're outside your orders,
now if you will please leave us be
we may move the horses by morning

<u>The Nettle Stings</u>

This is one from when a few of us trekked from crackly wood protection camp near Kenilworth to Poors' Piece near Steeple Claydon. I was flag carrier.

We were pretty much just following the estimated HS2 line pitching up in people's gardens and the such, once we had assured people we weren't gypsies, people were usually pretty nice. We got cake. We only really dealt with the law once and they were very friendly. I did obviously read them the poem. They liked it, and left.

*Massive amounts of bridleways closed due to the works is shocking, actually travelling the country on horseback *permissibly* is now very difficult indeed, if you have to stick to the A roads, 10 mile round trips and stuff are frankly shit scary. They are obviously supposed to provide diversions for these lost bridleways but they don't.*
So, some of these bridleways and small roads follow the landscape and have likely been walked by foot and hoof for a thousand years, but no longer.

<u>The Last On This Branch.</u>

I may be the last, to sit on this branch,
as the machines come rumbling in
I aim to delay,
the police will attend,
and tell me this crime is legal

These words became prophetic,
as we wandered past on horse
to build another roadway
to build another rail.

A stark, unpleasant reminder
that the rumbling never stops
and people have to fall asleep
and find something to eat
the police still say its legal,
this destruction of our woods
the systematic removal
of all the oldest living things

Where do we draw a balance
Where does a flag become a staff
Where do we draw a balance
between what is legal and what is right

<u>Not A Far Stones' Throw.</u>

Not a far stone throw
from civility and law
taxes and tickets
good manners and birds
lies a little place
where the police cast a shade
to do their dirty business
strip children to intimidate

Not all police are bastards
but Thames valley are thugs
who'll cut peoples safety lines,
to try and drown them in the drink
not all police are bastards
but not one should stand proud
when they stand in line with villains
corporatists and banks

When large men in violent groups
work under supervision of constabulary
they're not really protecting us are they?

They're tasers for hire,
cuffs for credit, batons for bank accounts
all the things you stand against
and pay your taxes for
such ironies may not be missed,
when the guillotines begin to fall

<u>Not A Far Stones' Throw</u>

Thames valley have been paid loads of money by HS2 and so are no way independent, Its savage. They have cut cables people are suspended on, sent up to 50 officers to directly facilitate wildlife crime. They strip search a load of under 18s in an obvious intimidation tactic against Denham camp.
They knew they were minors but were being "difficult" or "not entirely compliant to the whims of the officer present" so obviously that facilitates the necessity to commit what could be easily considered sexual violence against children

The police deal with all the terrible stuff in society and honestly don't get enough thanks about this, but they are an intrinsic part of the system that cause most of the problems they deal with. People who put on the uniform sacrifice the right to an opinion as soon as they put the funny hat on. Poor life choices. Not necessarily bastards.

I will convert the constabulary to well-rounded anarchists one poem at a time.

<u>Try</u>

Try and carve a bone a day,
and write at least two poems
not always an easy feat
for a full time anarchist activist.
bonus points if I don't get wet,
and keep all of my fingers
try and find a way to feed myself,
on something more than biscuits
try to drink more water,
don't get lifted by the police.

Try not to say anything that will make people cry,
try not to get angry about other peoples' lives
if you're asking where I'll be in five years
you haven't walked a path that teaches you
the rules of the world.

The certainty of uncertainty, is a bet I'll stake my life,
could you have thought a year ago
the government would make us wear masks
the only people that know
where they'll be in five years
are the poor bastards in the royal hotel
with ten more years to serve.

<u>Poems, Ponies And Protest.</u>

Poems, ponies and protest,
by people who perceive what you are yet to see,
moving down a line
where the carnage has been booked in.
village by village, mile by mile
I'm yet to speak to a single human
who hasn't hanged their head and sighed

"But what are we to do?
against such a massive plan
the government has stamped it
and we are but the people"

People are the power I cry, I've seen it and I've done it
I have watched the government fail,
when trying to suppress us
a hundred people arm in arm
get whatever they want that day
a thousand people camped in a town
get it for two weeks
ten thousand people on a march
can force a government twisting their arm.
a million not paying their taxes,
will bring those bastards to heel.

People are the power and we're rising day by day
we're not marching for small changes
we're marching for it all.
if you want to know how to do it
come join us as we walk.

<u>Free Days</u>

Some days I want to write, some days I want to climb
some days I want nothing but to hide myself and cry
I rarely do the latter, I often do the first
but I live a life of freedom
where I can do exactly
as I wish

All my sorrows for the captives
chained to desk and screen
my pity for the people
bound by bureaucracy
those wretches under the lash
of rush hours, schedules and clock
I hope to set at least one right
by telling them to stop

Take a leaf from the book of trees
and live a little more
like the creatures do
unplug yourself from the datastream
and find out what fulfils you

You'll understand what's precious
clean water, ripe fruit and heat
and probably more considering,
about what is left next year

Leave the towns and cities
abandon them to dust
live back in the forest
while there's still some forest left.
grasp back from freedom
if we still remember
what that is.

<u>Existence Is Resistance.</u>

Existence Is resistance, when you run counter to the grain
if you see that grain runs, towards a tragic end
a life of truth is protest, against the modern age
where post-truth fake news tries to convince you something not true

Existence is resistance, it's more effective than a fight
you can stop a billion pound machine
living on the right site
a life of song will save you, from the long slow death that occurs
by getting chipped away and paid a small wage
for someone else's gain

Existence is resistance, but it will come with its own strifes
you may be forced to speak to the police,
a little more than one might like
but doing what is right
means it's easy to sleep at night

Existence is resistance, you can do it every day
when someone tells you how to live
politely tell them, no

<u>Existence Is Resistance</u>

Saw a good banner some comrades were painting, got to talking.....

Fighting the system is hard. Our whole world is stacked to make it that way. Living in spite of it is much more enjoyable, Just ignore all the taxes and contacts, social media and breaking news.
Our society is focused on war, famine, pestilence, rumours of wars, greed, people being bastards, poor role models.

There is still good in the world, The TV just doesn't cover it.

To exist differently is the resistance.

<u>Saving A Single Tree</u>

Saving a single tree may seem insignificant
but many hands and many days,
may save the whole of a forest.

When people come together
to stand against the plans
that intend to scar the landscape
turn life into pennies and pounds

To do this work with humour
to undertake this task with love
is to set a good example
for all those stuck at home

It takes a day to save a tree
an hour to cut one down
a mission made much harder
by written laws that profoundly
miss the point

To save the world for everyman
to save the land for humankind
and all the other creatures
that fly, or tunnel, or crawl
is the whole reason we make rules, into laws.

Somewhere along the line, the intent was turned around
and rather than keeping us safe,
they have been bastardised to brutalise
any individual lacking in capital
if we paid the trees for making air
holding water and making soil
the law may then consider them
entities worth more than nothing

What's the cash value of the air you can breathe,
how much would you pay to prevent annual flooding
how many pennies for each leaf
that turns to mulch and grows your tea
what's the cost of bedding
for the birds and the bees

providing we can find the restraint
to ignore the gains
board rooms encourage
against ecologists' complaints

Every sapling's sacred, at a hundred and some years old
once a generation has sheltered
love has been made beneath
saving a single tree may seem insignificant
but I promise you it's not
every one of them matters
along with every patch of moss
these are the places that sustain us
these are the places we find God.

<u>Alone By The Fire</u>

Me and a bottle of port
sat alone by the fire
all the ones I love
are camped in fields
far from here

I sit, not lonely
but sombre
wondering if ever
they will come back

The bottle of port
ignores my witty retorts
and works to make me drowsy
the fire of course
gives warm hugs
but is eternally hungry

I'm sheltered in my shack
I've got food to last a month
but as the rain begins to fall
I've no one to play cards with.

My quandary is this
do I feed the fire
and drink the rest
or do I crawl off
to sleep in my nest

Perhaps the port and warmth
will inspire a wonderous lyric
or a life changing meditation
on how the stars work

Or perhaps it just means
another wood run
and an empty bottle
to make my head hurt in the morn

<u>Banged in Some Nails</u>

Banged in some nails and did some living
made a place to try and fix things
stop terrible crimes
when the cops are clueless
work out ways they can't just shoo us

When you're aware what's lost
cannot be repaired
and raising the alarm on Facebook
isn't getting shared

What can you do but turn up and boo
glue yourself to the padlocks
dig a hole and hold true
with heart and ingenuity
experience and youthful flame
and a sense of justice
that knows what's to blame

A brave and cosy number unknown
they're holding on tightly
they're digging for victory
so valiant and vindicated
they're caged in by bailiffs
barking like the ministers' hounds
to drag them out the ground
to build a fucking taxi rank

<u>A Creaky Tower</u>

We built a creaky tower
fashioned between two oak
four bed with penthouse
locking doors and good views

But the sharks are circling
ever tighter around
with orders, claims
and eviction demands

The hammer is hovering above

We built a creaky tower
with wood and string and hope
it's a place we can fight our war
without ever leaving bed
Careful of your footing
and never cut that rope

Our tower is for the anarchists
who sleep by tarp and board
our tower is for the trees it's on
To prevent them being killed
our tower is for the people
who protect the trees and moss

There are no rules,
no pets, no police
and you can climb
if you're in on the joke

<u>Day 3</u>

Day 3, I'm far away
the chariot has failed us
so we watch the war on the web
from our phones
charged by the same cold wind
that's just whipped down our friends

There tree tops are bare
of people who care
the last to climb them
vandals
saw in hand
who will bring those ancient creatures
down

And those that dig for victory
they now have my prayers
when bailiffs work in shifts
to make sure they stay scared
but those souls are fearless
I know them to attest this

They put their lives on the line
for those they'll never meet
they face the gravest fears for those
who are likely ignorant
that because of some bright brave souls
their lives could go on.
they're down there for all of us
and the authorities are brutal

Wake the fuck up London
next it could be you

*This was written on the third day of the Euston gardens tunnel eviction.
they manged to hold out for a month, amazing people.
Go badgers!*

*Digging a tunnel that takes the authorities a month to shift you from in zone 1 of
London city is a pretty amazing feat.*

Glory is in the sky, victory is in the dirt.

<u>Leaky Hovel</u>

Date's the 23rd
and I sit in my leaky hovel
ravens flown to get the booze
so I'm almost set for Christmas

I've chopped half a ton of firewood
in the pissing rain
I've come in to put the kettle on
and write what's in my brain

The tempo of the rain is exciting
and the December gloom
gives our wood an eerie look
for when duck comes for dinner

I sit in my leaky hovel
and I'm as happy as a pig
in the proverbial paradise
where pork is no longer purchased

I've fire, food and wine
we can dine by candle light
our table is our canvas
the walls are our art
blessed and lived in space
are more than a little dry spot

I sit in my leaky hovel
I've shored it up with more sticks
tipped the ponds out from the roof
moved the bedding to where we roost

We made it with pallets for pennies
and a few broken sticks
and if the bailiffs come next month
I'm going to terribly miss it

Off The Rails

There was that time the police came
and stole my precious staff
I'd been gifted by a wounded wood
and carried it on foot

From the camp of ours by the northline
to a central moot
the authorities were quick
to stamp the embers in our hearth
the first morning I awake
to chaos and alarm

Section 61
reserved for special times
when there is violence or aggression
things we left behind

An unauthorised encampment
is not against the law
we demand somewhere to meet
it is our right
it is the law

My pleas were met with repetition
40 officers and a digger
I battered them with poetry
they responded with cuffs
they chased away our horses
they threw us in the road
they pulled down our speaking place
they bulldozed our home

Then they tried to jail me
but it was their crime not mine
they had no right to drive us
from the land we occupied.

<u>Off The Rails</u>

This was about a time we had organised to have a little get together on an abandoned rifle range, The police, not really having any reason to be involved at all., decided to grab the nearest bit of paper that sounds like it has something to do with us and wave it about until everyone left.

I however read the paperwork. It was fucking nonsense and was not applicable to us in any way.
still they turned up in force with all the bells and whistles until they had intimidated everyone off the site.

I decided to dig my heels in and climb a tree. Took the wankers 3 hours to get me down and they ended up sticking me in the bucket of a private digger doing the whole "forward a bit, backwards a bit" on the radio. It was a shitshow

They gave me bail conditions they used in the broadest sense to inhibit me protesting (illegal) it was all related to HS2 yet the site we were moved from had nothing to do with them. So again. Pretty obviously targeted (illegal)

I spoke to a judge for under 5 mins (3 months later) and he threw it because it was obviously not lawful.

quality policing.

breaking articles 5,6,7,8 and probably 9 of the EU conventions on human rights. And totally in contradiction to the right to assemble and plan effective peaceful protest as enshrined in UK law

<u>The People Of Poors' Piece</u>

We are the people of Poors' Piece
here to protect the poors' last bit

Planted with trees
by men wiser than we
So people with nothing
have somewhere to live

Land kept well
by well-meaning lords
who understood their lives
were not the lives of all

Oak and elm and rising ash
housing bats and mice and kites
and kept as a place
to find some peace
when the village inn
became too intense

And now we are forced
to pitch our tents
because a paper company
wants it for pence
all as part of a giant con
to rob the poor of all they've got

So help us please with string and cake
support us as we stand against
bailiffs backed by billions of pounds
to be extracted in toil
from your grand daughters
and sons.

<u>Kill This Company</u>

We can kill this company with a thousand cuts
this unstoppable force we can grind to a halt
we can do by standing unflinching like iron
or by rising like the flood plains there on.

Sneaking into land they'll steal
that they don't need to lay rails
and building villages for people who are lost
in this evolving age that is upon us

Things they should work around
considering their promises
to the public trail
and they must tell MPs of town
exactly how many
old trees cut down

Dig in hard and dig in deep
live your lives in spite of deeds
that were stolen from honest hands
and given to crooks, greedy for land.

Where territory is disputed
make moving us harder
than the alternative

By saving bits that shouldn't be lost
we can drive up the cost
until they realize the price to be paid
isn't worth it for another fucking train

<u>Spycop Crimes</u>

Security culture and spycop crimes
justify paranoia in modern times
when legislation allows murder
to dig out crimes
society is in disorder

Asking questions, You're a cop.
Making plans, You're a cop.
Everyone's a cop
even when they're not

There is no amount of leverage
the authorities can't obtain
so it's easy to fall badly
into the grassing game

When paranoia's justified
how do you survive

How can you not imagine
how they justify to themselves
money, love of country
or freedom from the cells.

Everyone's the thought police
your powerless to resist
eventually you'll conclude
you're the only one
not an agent

When paranoia's justified
how do you survive

Stand tall, be proud
find your worth in your heart
cause no undue suffering
no distress or alarm

Speak your truth openly
and let the world see
tell them I am not a villain
tell them I am me

<u>A Policemen Told Me The Other Day</u>

A policeman told me the other day,
you're allowed one fundamental right a day
either you have the right to protest
or the right to food and rest

They say its fine, you can pick any time
dignity or safety, Speech or privacy
UK 98 human rights are great
means afterwards we may compensate
but we will ignore them on the day

The police are there to facilitate
for whatever their boss wants that day
the bailiffs are there to hurt you
because the man that pays them says to

Rights are things you argue
on your day in court
come the claims from the officer
paid to uphold law.

<u>Nervous Laughter</u>

The sound of laughing and banging hammers
dawn till dusk and through dark hours
Tins on ropes and water jugs
for when we flee to the trees
to read poetry

The police it seems, have taken sides
But our side is the chaos that is life
we harmonise and syncopate
together we do things that are great

With determination to stay upbeat
despite the plans of Tracy
the PLO from the British transport police
who sneered when she asked
if we were ready
for the illegal eviction
happening tomorrow

With laughs and loves
and sharing things
we're toe to toe with the man
with the magic money tree
If his money can fix any strife
then why are we a thing
when people start to protest
Perhaps those in power
should listen

<u>The Attack On Poors' Piece</u>

At five forty five
the militia rushed the ground
destroyed the poetry on the fences
and cut the draw bridge down

And laid a road
to bring their long necked machine
cut the ropes on rat
and left goldilocks to the rescue

By half two the day seemed long
despite the winter light
Our frustration emanates in waves
twisting aluminium frames
and rising in chants from people
who stay true
despite the sleepless anxieties
they are put through

Fifteen flavours of uniform
Still not a clue
a quarter click is what they grasped at
five meters what they stole
ripping roofs and spoiling food
we are not surprised it's true

It's a shame that we expect this
from forces forged for good
that have been puppetized
to dance an evil jig

At half four the first snake of the law
consisting of 8 poor fools in uniforms
slithered its' way from our wounded wood
to meet their masters on the hill

My heart beat races
as I'm caged out by fences
because they left us with the kitchen
and ignored my bastion

We cheer while they sneer at us

A last dance with the trees
before they destroy them
our song birds call
echoes through hearts
and puts warmth
when bailiffs have kicked out the hearth

At five fifteen they try to break physics
by taking the legs from out of our familys' nest
where some number,
sit squashed like sardines
scared and excited
and all in between

Already they are marking the trees they will kill.

When it rains aggressive men
who kick in windows
and stamp on your head
what is a human to do
when the police are stood there
watching
sipping a brew

Day 2 feels like a week in
so rapid the chipping
of our woods
it's a sin
you can ask
why I cry
for the dropping of dead trees
because the space they create
is home for miracles that live

Flying mammals that echolocate
silent birds that see at night

the authorities would only treat
our beaten brother oak
if all the other leaves
shielding the tree
would fall to the ground
and let the chainsaws inside

The hydraulic great axe
arrives from the east
and begins to feast
on the woods i call home
that I share
with badgers and voles

I sit later on a new ragged edge
on branches that hang sadly
over tin fence
I'm barred from my garden
by violent men

We sang songs from history
where the bailiffs got burned
and know that solidarity can turn
around our sick society
and make a better world
where humans are free

I'm in deep melancholy
in the crook of my tree
and I see 19 glaring at me
the oppressor slaves
trapped in uniform
for an hourly rate
betraying any decency
they try to hold
bailiffs are bastards
it's not a debate
but everyone can choose
to do something different
each day

Day 3 they brought down
the old boundary homes
reset the limits
on what the landless own
came and fenced our food garden
and only gave the buckets back
after they had shoved everyone about

Still they lurk on their fallback line

And I plant willow whips in hope
that this time, finally
they will stick to laws that are wrote

We're still vigilant
in the iron tower
the poet tree
still keeping an eye
through all hours
we've double the fires
the kettle is hot
we feed ourselves
and count what we've got

At one thirty
we have guests from the west
they lament the tragedy in their lands
and thank us for the things we can stand

Day 4 I'm appalled
at the rate trees fall
the aggressors that attack our wood
wont even leave the timber, for the soil

21,19 and 17 know we can hinder
promise they are not the ones
that beat and break fingers

Papers and promises
are quickly forgotten
when one can take advantage
of passive police
and the staff to do thuggery
get the job done
not give a fuck about casualties

My right ear hears
the singing of birds
to my reckoning
the wrens sound hopeful
in a choir of their community
that includes a handful
of red list species

But translated from avian
whose words are usually alien
they are pleading
for the destruction to stop

They cannot see why
the funny monkeys
who they share
their branches with
that leave them food
and are trusted under nests
cannot stop these other apes
in yellow and black
not like their friends
in camo and funny hats

they cannot see
the train line
their mind is confined
to what is real
they cannot see
the money change hands
in far away lands
that makes plans
to destroy and call it
progress.

They see them
trample the low perches
cover the worm forage in matts
rip down all the tarps
the sweet beetles hid at

They brought crashing down the world
of any tree dwelling creature
that called oak or poplar home.

The rarest of stems
vandalised and stolen
despite the cries
and legal papers from Clive
and promises to be good neighbours

and recreate nature
and not just be organised crime

Agencies I've never heard of.
with apparently more power than God
but the primary power being
40 odd strong fellas with cuffs
and presumably some training
and not just thugs
shipped in by the train full

The one that looks like
Ross Kemps' little brother
is up and down with his tempers
swearing and glaring
sometimes seeming to slow
but always prowling
up and down
the new fence like a hound
moments from tearing the throat
from a lamb

With little sleep
and no charged clock
I measure time
by trees that are dropped
the crash of each tall creature
hits me where I breathe
the shake trembles
through the soil
and up the iron tower
where I cower
from the mechanised ecocide
that's happening a stones throw
from my window

My left ear is the sounds that I fear
shouting work crews with engines and trucks
the screaming of our people
hurt again
when our groovy boy
was leapt on again
by a large man

Who hit him again
crushed his phone again
and laughed

It was all for his safety he was told
another round of violence against us
the utter hypocrisy of authorities
is still shocking every time

Day 5 I've slept
and we're still alive
spoken about the future
amongst ourselves and with Clive
the vandals have retreated
due to weekend shifts
but there are still 20 odd carrots
who are not allowed to sit
our woods chatter
with birdsong and pipes
playing songs about peoples' strifes

I sit in the crown
of our bold oak tower
our clove field is clear
but the bit they stole
is already scarred by tyres

Another shift arrives
as I watch the sun die
over a horizon
that's rapidly changing

The full moon rises in the sky
to replace the sleeping sun
I see the lunar disc fractured by branches
with an early orange glow

The sharks are still swimming
amongst the speechless carrots
talking about how best
to press onwards
into land where I stand
that they have no right to

Early evening gets exciting
when they're fighting over the fence
I don't mean with us about boundaries
I mean amongst themselves.

Days six through nine
I didn't write a line
looted and vandalised
abandoned by the crowds
too busy tidying
and trying to remediate
what was left
of our woodland
conservation project.
as March marches on.

Coombes came and vandalised my garden
four or five lads
with ropes and machinery
three or four cop types
retired from army
and twenty-five little people
told to keep eyes on the boundary

They have shored up the fence just enough
for me to think they will no longer push
however the leaning tree
of a now much rarer breed
is under threat,
from vanity and greed

The stem from which I watched
the kites hatch and play
all these men managed by lunch
was to climb and kick the nest away

They dropped limbs on my bins
with some sorry promise to replace it
like the promise to give the logs back
or turn the lights around
or be careful as they could
with our historic ancient wood

Oh poor josh.
he's stuck up a tree by someone who's angry
and the things he does for money
a role he chose,
and turns up for
and doesn't care
about the damage
and havoc that happens
when he's chainsawed all the trees away

A slave in his system of bosses and wage
doesn't understand he's sustaining his cage
thinks that he is lucky
to give up his autonomy
when it comes to where you eat
or what time you wake
or what forests you rape

He'll risk his life
for a chairman with a map
and will believe him
over the eyes under his hardhat

Oh poor josh,
out on a limb
because a fella in a machine teased him
and asked if he would keep complaining
the tree was shattering
into three foot splinters
or that dead children parents
keep crying and sighing
at the things he does for money

Like cutting the memorial
for all those sick kids
or laying low the stems
where our grandparents kissed
or kicking out the bird nests
just because he can

Day 91 climbed down
I capitulated to the man
we let them cut the head

of our quirky poplar stem
that had its roots in our home
but stretched out over the fence

Day 10 and they're done
finished raining sawdust on me
finished with being unkind
and ripping down vines
and flooding with light
these woods where the owls hide

Those precious perches on our edge
the texture of soil the trees had made
poplar, oak and people nests
sterilised by violence
to plastic and fence.

<u>The Attack On Poors' Piece.</u>

February 23rd, it was a Tuesday.

We had unofficially known it was coming,
They had built an attack ramp over the old railway, set up a massive gazebo and
equipment stores and a carpark over the old willow coppice.

However, we had no official notice, not even a note on the door.
Because of the whole covid "thing" evictions were supposed to be suspended, so
really, they shouldn't have been able to throw us out of any of the sites we were
living on during the lockdowns.

We were probably in the exemptions from that being a protest camp on
(debatably) HS2 land however that would still defer to the housing act. Which
gives minimum 14 days' notice, blah blah blah.
Its pretty pointless learning all the law about something when the authorities turn
up and don't give a fuck about it.

Tracey. Fucking Tracey. The scab on a scab, Police liaison officer from the British
Transport Police.
I saw her the day before she was getting the popcorn out, pretended not to hear any
legal complaints and was mocking us in a tone that really hit me.

"You ready for it?"

Tracey doesn't give a shit about what's legal or what's right, she's done her 30 years
and she's off soon, Thinks the police federation should be scrapped. I mean holy shit.

It is still shocking.

Same old story really. Only with a twist.
they would have come for the whole wood, or at least the camp.
however, the legal limbo of their boots on the ground Vs the legal maps
with a combination of a fuck off iron tower, and some incredibly resilient people on
the ground. Means they only got a strip of the woods.

That assault on that strip was brutal. A bailiff dropped from cranes to the high
house kicked in the windows and stamped all over people. Leaving injured
protestors stranded and then refusing to even facilitate his extraction without
everyone else giving up the house. It was levering a mans wellbeing after a vicious
assault to force people to give up their protest.

Even after the lines were decided and the kitchen was safe,
it was an eerie place to try and live,
trying to tidy up the damage and the mess,
still chopping wood and carrying water
but now under floodlights
and with 20 security staring at my bedroom 24/7
waiting for me to come out for a piss in the early hours.

Did our best to try and save what we could.
The wooded is wounded, but its alive.

I wish I managed to save the kites nest.

Coombes are cowboys
and their climbing is shit.

<u>Dear Carrots.</u>

It's easy to be party to a crime
when there's nothing else left to do
all the other works dried up
and the government throws you a rope

It's easy to be party to a crime
when all the information is compartmentalised
and the only information you have got
is you get twelve quid an hour
to stand by a fence

It's easy to be party to a crime
when it looks like digging hole
man who moved a hundred ton
gets two ton a day
but Bojos mate who cleans the machines
gets a hundred grand in two days

It's easy to be party to a crime
when a man with a clipboard says its fine
to turf badgers onto the road
bulldoze three hundred years of their homes

Can we expect everyone in a hardhat
to understand the critical importance of bats
resting, nesting and feasting on pests
from trees that have done
two hundred years of times test

Its easy to be party to a crime
when a political party says its grand
and keeping you in fulfilling work
is reason enough to rob some other poor sod

Fence off land and leave crops to rot
steals people right to graze their stock
and creating incomprehensible amounts of debt
that they will take back
from your twelve quid wage.